Contents

Foreword

Walter Hood embraces a unique perspective of the urban landscape. Artist, architect, landscape architect, writer, university professor, community resident, he is also, as is revealed in *Urban Diaries*, a sensitive observer and an articulate scribe. Illuminating the everyday rituals of his urban community of West Oakland, California, he bears witness to the humanity and complexity of inner city life. As a result of his ardent commitment to designing relevant, functional, and artistically vital urban spaces, Hood proposes an approach of innovative responsiveness to the needs of disenfranchised, neglected, isolated neighborhoods, tackling the core issues most often left out of contemporary design consideration.

Hood delivers his position as insider and observer with layered expressions unified in his own eloquent voice. To achieve familiarity, he puts himself *in* the community to see who the people are and his own connections to them, what they are doing, what their needs are, and what the flow of change discloses. His theoretical remedies encourage us to see the urban landscape with fresh and changed eyes. By offering his vision as an accessible example of an individual confronting problems creatively, Hood inspires others to find their own imaginative insights to forge new solutions for old problems.

—Leah Levy
Independent art curator
Berkeley, California

Preface

Looking out onto the streets from my window, I am aware of the paradox surrounding my residency here in West Oakland, California. I live and work in a light-filled loft studio in a rehabilitated laundry-service building. A remote controlled gate and brick walls separate my complex from the street. I am at ease when I move about the neighborhood, yet I've chosen to live in a secured environment. It would be foolish to suggest that my fear doesn't arise when sirens and gunfire wail, or that timidity doesn't surface when I'm out alone at night. Yet on most days and nights I feel safe. I wonder whether I will always live this way. Will time open my eyes to see these conflicting circumstances more clearly, or will I just leave?

In 1991 I began keeping daily journals as the method of recording my impressions of neighborhood events and activities. As time passed, I became part of the neighborhood, primarily in the role of observer and scribe. My vision is now clear, and the journal entries are an outlet for expression. The more I observe, the more I begin to wonder about my role in the community. The journal entries manifest my experiences and dreams.

Highly praised by planners in the late 1960s, the Model Cities Urban Revitalization Program focused on improving the physical and social environment of blighted portions of major United States cities. The program's primary goal was defined as "slum eradication." The community of West Oakland, California, was awarded Model Cities status in 1970, entitling it to receive funds for physical programs meant to revitalize the neighborhood. Amidst considerable fanfare, broad swaths of its "blighted" neighborhoods were demolished to make way for blocks of new low-income housing, neighborhood parks, and "open space." Revisiting West Oakland today, those "solutions" from the Model Cities Program are still visible, yet ironically, twenty-five years later, the community is again considered a "blighted" area, ripe for redevelopment by the City of Oakland Planning Department. The parks, open spaces, and housing projects that were created under the Model Cities Program have, almost without exception, become public nuisances: turf for illicit activity and targets of repeated vandalism.

If looked at solely in terms of their design response, the designers of the Model Cities Program, who relied heavily on data from demographic profiles, were handicapped in the face of the dynamic economic, physical, and social structures of the neighborhood. The standardized and one-dimensional environments generated by these quantitative models rarely met the demands of the communities they were intended to serve. In contrast, improvisation creates a direct link between theoretical planning and real community issues. Acting as both commentary and research, the improvisation process expresses particular attitudes about place and culture from an insider's view. The framework for inquiry begins with context: social and physical history and demographic change. Next, photo documentation, site inventories, postoccupancy evaluation, and daily journal entries recording social and cultural patterns fully bring the human condition into the design process. This process of inquiry allows social and cultural patterns to be transformed into physical form. It raises hard questions and responds to them with improvisational design strategies that bring us face-to-face with real issues in our urban communities.

Improvisation

Although improvisation operates within the environmental design tradition, it involves a unique design process. Improvisational design is the spontaneous change and rhythmic transposition of nonobjective compositions and traditional design elements within a spatial field created by a distinct framework (classical or abstract). Change and transpositions are guided by individual expression, combined with social, environmental, and political multidisciplinary analysis, traditional design strategies (such as composition and scale), and an understanding of common, everyday objects and practices (which I will refer to as "familiar"). These nonobjective compositions are free of programmatic constraints: they are silent forms and compositions awaiting identity. In the context of improvisation, existing design archetypes and traditional forms are reshaped into new and unique forms through the incremental transfer of ideas to provide familiar objects in space, reinforcing the image of the community, and extending the tradition. The process of improvisation clearly departs from the notion of a specific design hegemony, and it positions the designer within an environment for creativity. As a method of inquiry, improvisation generates a new series of goals:

1. Spontaneous change as a cultural norm—Cities and communities are in constant flux, and places should be adaptive and allowed the freedom of individual or community expression.
2. The expression of self—The designer is not relegated to the role of facilitator or planner, but gives formal interpretations.
3. Reinforcing the image of the community—The familiar validates the existence of multiple views of life in the city, even those that are outside the normative view.
4. Extending and enriching the tradition of environmental design—Improvisation utilizes previous canons as a framework for departure, but demands individual responses. It promotes change by concentrating on the collective and individual familiarity for each component in relationship to the specific place or culture. The familiar unfolds in the invention of particular elements, spatial relationships, or patterns derived from particular practices that reflect attitudes and values over time.

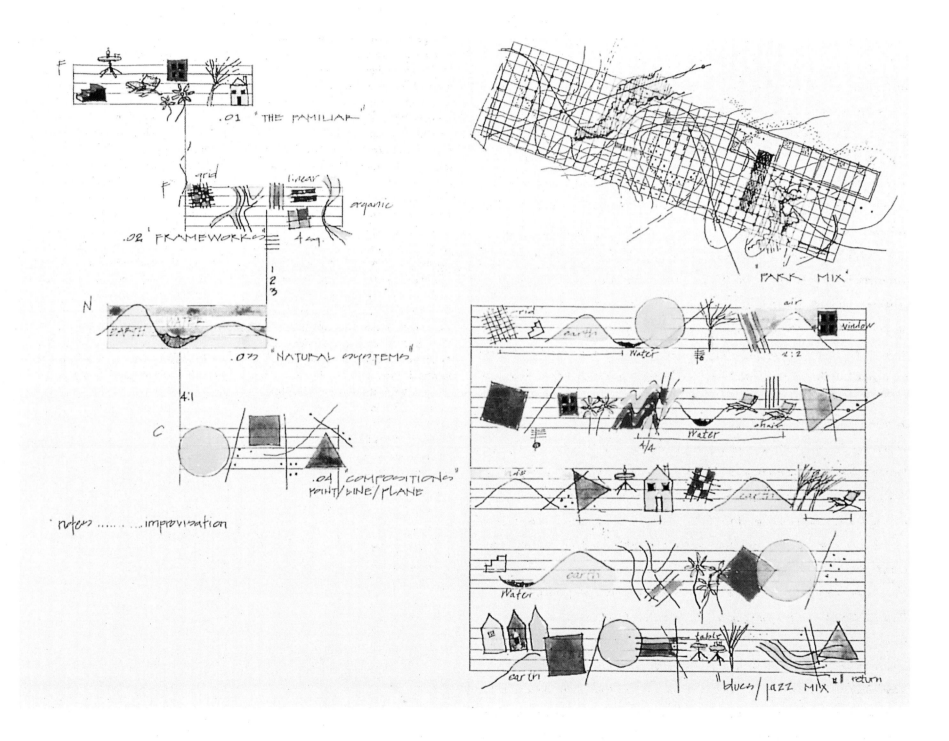

The Familiar

For each design component, the "famil-iar" must be uncovered, stimulating the designer to create new designs that are particular. Sociologist Herbert Blumer theorizes that "all objects are social products in that they are formed and transformed by the defining process that takes place in social interaction. The meaning of the objects—chairs, trees—is formed from the ways in which others refer to such objects or act towards them."[1] A familiar practice or object might be highly valued in one culture, while, in another, it might be com-pletely nonexistent. The *familiar* recog-nizes that space is "egocentric," varying from individual to individual. The Improvisation Diagram illustrates this process in the form of sheet music. The "familiar" has dialogue with each design component, resulting in a design process similar to the structure of jazz music. Design components act as rhythms, combining and restructuring elements and spaces in the search for *familiarity* to place and culture. They begin and end within the boundary of the site. Multiple responses are layered, formu-lating a gestalt, which Schultz defines as a "structure, configuration, or pattern of physical, biological, or psychological phenomena so integrated as to consti-tute a functional unit with properties not derived by the summation of its parts."[2] The result is the creation of familiar objects in space. These objects cannot be read in their entirety, but they function through their interrela-tionships, their uses, and the meanings users attach to them. New forms, elements, and patterns are inclusive in the integrity and meaning of the design.

The Urban Landscape

In his writings on community building, architect Lars Lerup explains: "To begin a new environment demands an understanding of both the existing and the past. It is a multidimensional under-standing, made up of the social, personal, political, economic and physical. . . ."[3] Lerup's dictum serves as my point of departure, suggesting "improvisation" as a research tool to evaluate and respond to the multidimensional phenomena that influence and define the design of our communities. Improvisation establishes a holistic process of inquiry, including daily journal entries recording observations, postoccupancy evaluation of design interventions, demographic profiles, patterns of use, interviews, site inventories, social and physical history, and photographic documentation.

The exploratory research summa-rized here focuses on a common phenomenon in the United States urban landscape: the minipark. The urban minipark is most often found in inner city neighborhoods that were redeveloped during the 1960s and 1970s. As a pragmatic extension of what soci-ologist Galen Cranz defined as the open space movement's scramble for land in cities, planners and advocates treated the minipark as a valuable commodity, a means to secure needed public space in urban areas. "Competition for land, particularly with freeways and housing, was greater than ever before, so open space ideology rationalized the minipark, the play lot, and the vest pocket park, parks that could be tucked into irregular, unusual, inexpensive sites that had been rejected in prior eras."[4] You can find urban miniparks in most U.S. cities, and their form and design look remarkably similar no matter what city you visit.

Typically, the minipark's elements are simple: an open green area (serpentine in form) augmented with standardized amenities such as benches, game tables, drinking fountains, manufactured play environments, and, occasionally, court areas for basketball, handball, tether ball, and so forth. Underlying these standard forms and programmatic elements are social reform tactics, allowing only normative or mainstream use of spaces and infrastructure.

Programmed for specific activities and providing alternative recreational activities for particular groups of people, the minipark is a structured environment. On occasion, adults or older siblings bring small children to play at the park. But more commonly, groups of school-age children *en route* to various scenes of entertainment and activity in the neigh-borhood stop for a while in the park. A few teens, with no other place to go, perch along the minipark's benches, scoping the street. A pickup game of basketball on the half court enlivens the park on a warm evening.

Other people use the urban minipark too, but their needs subvert the site's implicit program. We see other uses every day: homeless adults enjoying conversation and a drink, neighborhood recyclers taking their shopping carts into the park to rest for a bit, teenagers expressing themselves through tagging and graffiti. The formula for the urban minipark is set within guidelines and standards. Its form and context attempt to predetermine events and uses. Thus, although the minipark serves some chil-dren and teens, it leaves other segments of society without a sense of legitimate right to use the space. Social injustices are created when certain uses are ignored or not provided for in the park, sometimes causing conflicts when unprogrammed uses occur.

Conflict between programmed and unprogrammed uses of community facilities raises critical questions for designers, particularly in urban neigh-borhoods. For example, as public space in the ever-privatized urban environment becomes scarce and financial budgets of public agencies dwindle, how can amenities such as these miniparks be redesigned to serve the community more effectively? Historically, the values and attitudes that have shaped these spaces have been derived from outside, middle-class values. What strategies would better allow the voices of the community residents to be heard? When designers recreate public spaces according to familiar practices and patterns of neighborhood people, will a different set of values, attitudes, and forms unfold? And, finally, should people be allowed to dream: "How can *my* needs be met in the public places of *my* community?"

The theoretical redesign of three urban miniparks in West Oakland, California, illustrates how a design process can open to new levels of community awareness and empower-ment. As originally designed, these parks epitomized the neat packaging of mainstream morality, which is made physical through institutional, standard-ized design. The proposed redesigns, though theoretical, offer pragmatic ways of viewing and investigating without false moralism or standardization. They illustrate how disenfranchised communities can be part of the process of reconstructing their public environment. Throwing away irrelevant notions, moral stances, and reformist approaches to design is essential if a public space is truly to serve its community. The improvisational process, therefore, juxtaposes the historical remnants with the contemporary rhythms of everyday life, in order to facilitate a fresh approach that allows the designer's eyes and ears to be open to the community. Historical research is familiar to most designers; observation of everyday life is not. Yet, as landscape architect Randy Hester writes, observation "is the single best technique for discovering what people do and how people interact with other people in neighborhood space." [5]

The research for this study has been organized in the form of a diary of daily personal observations. Scenarios of everyday experience were witnessed and documented as narrative: from the old men sitting in the park telling stories to children of single mothers who have no time to take their children to the park, to the entrepreneurial activities of automobile detailing at the park's periphery, to the daily routines of local prostitutes. Each activity, event, or circumstance becomes a revelation. A multitude of voices can be heard. Some had the attention of park planners twenty-five years ago; others, then as now, were neglected and ignored. Diary entries and narrative express the mood and character of the community and elicit an improvisational response. Observation and self-reflection inspire programming based on user-needs, which are transformed into design interventions.

The reader needs an open mind to understand the diaries. A willingness to accept new and different information is key to creating new urban landscapes. No attempts are made to conform to institutional policies or political positions. The neighborhood is the client, one that has been voiceless in determining how formal public spaces are designed.

Biography and Demographics

The three parks examined in this book, Durant Minipark, 25th Street Park, and Grove Shafter Park, are situated in a predominately African American neighborhood on the easternmost edge of West Oakland, California. Before we can attempt to understand the issues surrounding these open spaces in West Oakland, we must first attempt to define the city's neighborhoods and their corresponding myths. As city planner Thomas Angotti summarizes, "Neighborhoods are both myth and reality. As reality, they are objective phenomena that arise from metropolitan growth within particular economic and historical context. Their character and problems reflect the social and economic systems within which they flourish. However, there is also a subjective aspect of neighborhood development. Every neighborhood is, to a greater or lesser degree, a myth that evolves in the collective consciousness of its people." [6]

West Oakland hosts several smaller neighborhoods within its boundaries. Each of these is physically, politically, and socially unique. But, in the collective consciousness of residents, they are all tied to the greater neighborhood's myths and realities. Historical analysis offers a view into the neighborhood's origin as a single geographic entity, allowing us a better understanding of the events and changes that have shaped the subjective views of its inhabitants.

The physical geography that defines each minipark's immediate neighborhood illustrates its isolation within the larger West Oakland context. Oakland's major arterials radiate northwards from its Central Business District: Telegraph Avenue to the east and San Pablo Avenue to the west. These arterials establish boundaries for this small neighborhood. Martin Luther King Jr. Way, another arterial, runs parallel between Telegraph and San Pablo Avenues. The neighborhood is dramatically isolated from Oakland's Central Business District by the elevated eight-lane freeway and by the elevated tracks of the Bay Area Rapid Transit (BART). San Pablo Avenue creates a sharp edge to the west, separating the specific neighborhood from greater West Oakland. In effect, BART, the freeway, and the major arterials create a medieval fortress wall, isolating the community from the adjacent downtown area and the greater community.

Such physical fragmentation was not always the situation in this neighborhood. Sanborn Insurance Maps from 1902, 1929, and 1950, combined with census data, archival research, and interviews with older residents, reveal substantial neighborhood change. Stages of the neighborhood's physical transformation are illustrated in the following statistics.

West Oakland, California

9

1902

Major Events

In 1869, Oakland was chosen as the western terminus for the Southern Pacific Railroad's transcontinental route. Shortly before this event, the Pullman Company had introduced its sleeping cars, which included the service of porters. The influence of the railroad and local industry imprinted West Oakland's physical and community environment with employment opportunities, while it also fostered segregation. "By company policy, the porter was a black man. At the end of the line, Oakland, which in 1870 counted fifty-five black residents, became home base to a growing number of Pullman Porters and their families."[7] West Oakland developed into a predominantly African American community. Historian Douglas Daniels notes that, as early as 1890, "groups of black San Franciscans adopted a suburban lifestyle by moving to the East Bay, where they enjoyed larger homes, more space for yards and children, and suffered less noise and congestion."[8] This style of life was commonly referred to as "Victorian."

Land Use

The West Oakland neighborhood hosted a large percentage of single-family residential houses, flats, boarding houses, institutional uses (primarily churches and clubs), and commercial uses. Opportunities for African Americans were not restricted at this time. "African Americans bought spacious houses in the East Bay, or comfortable dwellings in San Francisco. The less expensive East Bay homes freed portions of home owners' budgets to buy furnishings, plant flowers, and devote space for their children's play activities."[9]

Demographics

1870	10,500 total population
	55 black residents
1900	66,900 total population
	1000+ black residents

1929

Major Events

For African Americans, the Great Depression marked a significant change: the demise of economic opportunities in the East Bay. The high visibility of people loitering, urban farming practices in residential areas, and non-Victorian social patterns, exacerbated the perception of cultural differences between migrants and existing residents. But, during this time, West Oakland also blossomed, with blues and jazz clubs becoming very popular among both blacks and whites.

Land Use

Boarding houses, single-room hotels, and duplexes provided rental opportunities for migrants from the South and Midwest during the first two decades of the twentieth century. Institutions and commercial establishments, such as churches, YMCAs, and movie houses, sprang up to provide social services and recreation. The area benefited from good access to jobs located in bay-front industries and the downtown. By 1930, however, the West Oakland area was faced with overcrowding, insufficient housing, and declining employment opportunities. Residents began to improvise and reshape the urban landscape to fit their needs. "Old houses in West Oakland, sometimes without indoor plumbing and often suffering from lack of maintenance during the depression, were suddenly occupied by as many as fifty men, often sleeping in shifts of 'hot beds'."[10] The area quickly transformed from its Victorian era roots to a working-class neighborhood landscape.

Demographics

1930	284,063 total population
	10,000 African Americans

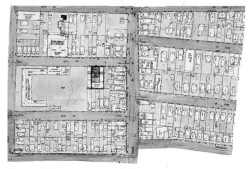

Durant Minipark 1902

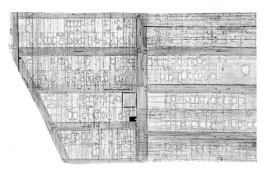

25th Street Park 1902

Grove Shafter Park 1902

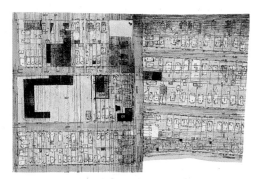

Durant Minipark 1929

25th Street Park 1929

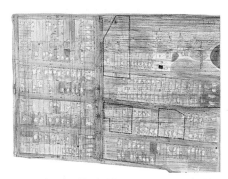

Grove Shafter Park 1929

1956

Major Events

In 1949, the Oakland City Council declared West Oakland a blighted area. This designation practically ensured that the area would become the target for widespread demolition in the name of progress.

By 1954, two hundred acres of land in West Oakland had been cleared of homes, businesses, and civic institutions under the Acorn Urban Renewal Plan. Over nine thousand people had been displaced. By the end of the decade, West Oakland, which had been a cultural and economic center for Oakland's African American community for three-fourths of a century, was virtually destroyed, its boundaries obscured, and its neighborhoods fragmented.

Land Use

By 1956, multifamily, middle-class, and subsidized housing dominated West Oakland's physical environment. Fewer than thirty percent of the population owned their own homes. Commercial uses diminished as supportive middle-income groups moved to neighboring suburbs.

Demographics

(1950 was the first year for specific census tract designation. The following figures illuminate demographics in the case study area of West Oakland.)

1950   25,764 total population
        64% African American
        34% white
        2% other

The area had a stable family community, with eighty-eight percent of the community consisting of families, seventy-five percent of which were married. The unemployment rate was sixteen percent.

1992 - Present Day

Major Events

The destruction of much of West Oakland's residential fabric coincided with the loss of low-income housing, predominantly serving African Americans, in adjacent communities. Overcrowding and an increase in the level of poverty in remaining affordable housing areas ensued. This phenomenon, coupled with the development of new suburbs, precipitated the flight of the wealthier segments of the population. This exodus further contributed to the decline of West Oakland by leaving it bankrupt of the wealth and diversity needed to sustain a thriving community. Once a working-class community with the physical and social infrastructure to sustain itself, by 1992 the neighborhood had become economically marginal, its physical edges splintered, and its social systems decaying. Remaining businesses were mostly liquor stores, check-cashing establishments, and fast-food restaurants.

Land Use

During the 1960s and 1970s, public housing replaced many multifamily institutions and apartment buildings. By 1992, home ownership declined further, with less than one in five neighborhood residents owning their own homes. Many local institutions, specifically churches and community centers, were demolished or moved away. The remaining cornerstone commercial shopping institution, Sears Roebuck, closed in 1993.

Demographics

1990   19,000 total population
        69% African American
        16% white
        15% other

The area is characterized by a breakdown in family structures. Fifty-one percent of the community consists of families. In only twenty-one percent of the families are the parents married. Female-headed households constitute the majority family structure. There is a doubling of the elderly population.

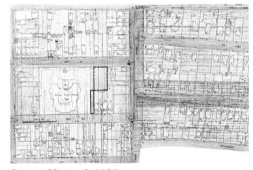

Durant Minipark 1956

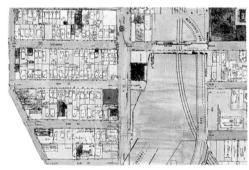

25th Street Park 1956

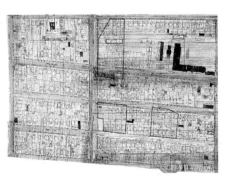

Grove Shafter Park 1956

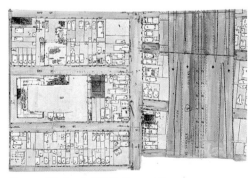

Durant Minipark 1992–Present Day

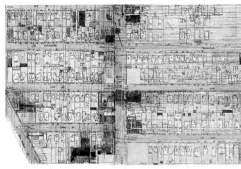

25th Street Park 1992–Present Day

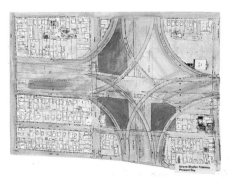

Grove Shafter Park 1992–Present Day

Interventions & Consequences

"The Model Cities Urban Revitalization Program, a new model for social reform and redevelopment in the late 1960s and early 1970s, was highly praised by planners, politicians, and community leaders. The program, utilizing federal dollars, launched a concerted effort to improve the socially, economically, and physically blighted neighborhood environments of major U.S. cities. In 1968 five Model Cities agencies in the Department of Housing and Urban Development (HUD) Region VI were operating in predominately black neighborhoods in Seattle, WA; Portland, OR; Fresno, Richmond and Oakland, CA." [11] In an effort to clean up blighted areas and provide city beautification, programs included tree planting, curb and sidewalk repair, improvements to existing parks, acquisition of new park land, and social services.

Oakland was awarded Model City money in 1970, and the West Oakland community was designated as a Model Neighborhood. The overall program plan as administered by HUD targeted social services, housing, city beautification, and park rehabilitation and improvements. This was criticized in initial stages: "The Model Cities lacks easily accessible and adequate indoor/outdoor recreational facilities and spaces needed to serve the range of different age groups residing in the area, particularly teenagers. In addition, it lacks the different kinds of smaller recreational areas more appropriate to the very young and aged," (Application for Planning Grant, Model Cities Program, City of Oakland, 1967). The Model Cities Program's solution to these problems entailed increasing the number of parks in the model neighborhood, improving the quality of existing social facilities, in staffing as well as physical appearance, and the construction of subsidized, low-income housing.

Much of this history has left remnants, marks, and scars on West Oakland's physical structure. The open spaces and housing projects that were created still exist. But these physical interventions did not end up as they were first envisioned. They have become under-utilized public nuisances and focal points of repeated vandalism. *They are mean landscapes.*

Economic infrastructure never materialized to support community development. In its place, incompatible and nuisance-generating enterprises have emerged. The systematic introduction of transportation infrastructure to the community's edges has further isolated the community, socially and economically, from the central city. West Oakland's demise is a typical tale of the fate of African American neighborhoods in urban America. "African American neighborhoods have historically been the most subject to removal by urban renewal, gentrification and housing abandonment; the federal urban renewal program became known as the 'Negro Renewal' in the 1960s." [12] West Oakland and its neighborhoods are a physical testament to these outside actions.

West Oakland's demise can be attributed in particular to the following factors:

The Model Cities Program and the Open Space movement relied heavily on social programming to provide human services in these communities. With cutbacks and the complete eradication of state and federal programs during the late 1970s and 1980s, these programs were left unsupported.

As city and neighborhood economic/physical/social structures were transformed, residents' values and needs changed. The standardized and one-dimensional environments that were created could not meet the changing demands of the communities.

Urban Diaries

The diaries present the observation of a wide variety of human experiences and suggest an equally wide variety of changes to West Oakland's miniparks and their context. Jane Jacobs observes that, "City parks are not abstractions, or automatic repositories of virtue or uplift, anymore than sidewalks are abstractions. They mean nothing divorced from their practical, tangible uses, and hence they mean nothing divorced from the tangible effects on them—for good or ill—of the city districts and uses touching them." [13] The diaries present a way to listen to the stories and lives of neighborhood residents and see the tangible elements that create the rhythms and soul of the community. They remarry residents to the landscapes they inhabit.

Transformations

With each diary entry, a new layer of utility is added and woven into the park producing a total of five functions and programmatic pieces. The design implications—explored in plans, sections, elevations, perspectives, axons, and models—of the new layers are direct translations of functional uses and observed events. By investigating each layer on its own terms, particularities and spatial patterns are resolved. From Day One (first layer) through Day Five (fifth layer), each set of issues and programmed events is carried forward, commingling with the next. This suggests an open-ended design process. Based on the use and values of the inhabitants, the design of each day can stand alone, or it can be combined with others in a series of expanding transformations.

The diaries begin . . . .

Study Areas

Durant Minipark—
The Mid-Block Park

Durant Minipark is a quarter-acre rectilinear site. It occupies a former house lot. The park is sandwiched between an elementary school and a pair of duplexes. The street's land uses are typically residential, with a variety of single-family homes, apartments, rooming houses, and artist studios. A corner liquor/grocery store and an adjacent four-lane arterial street are within easy visual and pedestrian access of the park. Only the front edge of the park is open to the street. Existing site elements include hardy eucalyptus trees and evergreen shrubs, manufactured play equipment, game tables, benches, and a drinking fountain.

Typically, the park is vacant most of the day. Apart from those stopping to drink *en route* from the corner store, the park has very few users. The play equipment, benches, and drinking fountain sit in the landscape like ruins, weathered by time and neglect. Durant Minipark appears to have been placed in the community by foreign hands. The large grounds of the school next door engulf the activities of local kids: basketball, track, baseball, tag, and just hanging out occur daily, whether school is in session or not.

Juxtaposing Durant Minipark's historic context with its current use allows the designer to propose interventions that result in the social, economic, and physical transformation of this space. The framework for design is a golden section, creating two squares of equal proportion which unfold out to the street. The diagram assures proportional distribution of form and space.

Durant Minipark

Day One

I've noticed this garden for a long time.
Always neat. Vegetables and roses
commingle, creating beautiful borders
along the sidewalk. Multicolored flowers
playfully contrast with the green lawn.
The water jugs along the path intrigue
me. Why are they there? My barber tells
me they keep dogs out. I've never seen
the gardener, but when I do, I'll ask him
or her about the jugs.

Gardening

Defined in this context as a place of cultivation and horticultural practices, the garden is the first programmatic layer. Raised planting beds are sited to take advantage of solar access, a grid of fruit trees coexists in direct confrontation, creating a path or line which leads to the utility structure. Herbs of various sorts proliferate along the site's edge. The primary requirement for the garden is human access, along with sufficient agricultural holdings for a minimum of ten families, one half the street's population. For those who want to participate, there would be ample space. Based on horticulturist Bruce Stoke's recommendation that a family of four can produce two-thirds of its vegetables on six hundred square feet of land, with five hours of cultivation time per week, [14] a six-thousand-square-foot space is required. The allotment is based on the probability that not all residents of the street will participate in the ritual of gardening. The garden is free from other uses in Day One; the space is reoriented to one dimension, serving those who want to cultivate.

The Garden

I never see more than one or two gardeners
in the garden at any time, but the plentiful
bounty reveals their labor and dedication.
Corn, collard greens, potatoes, and flowers
are planted densely in the raised beds.
Neighborhood kids have turned the storage
shed into a playhouse. When the gardeners
leave, the children play tag and hide-and-
seek amongst the vegetable beds.

15

Day Two

They never play on the old play equipment. When I pass by, I see them digging in the dirt or climbing the old sycamore tree. The chain-link fence has become a wave-maker and the sandbox seat wall is the forum for Simon Says. They never use the standardized play equipment, at least I don't see them.

Playground

The garden from Day One accepts the local children. The utility building becomes a clubhouse. Youth claim and inhabit this structure as part of their play. Seen as an architectural "lump" [15] of material, the building can be transformed through the children's imagination to become something like a starship or a fort. A sandbox is also added. These new elements serve as the starting point to investigate the play environment for children. The space accommodates both activities: gardening and children's games.

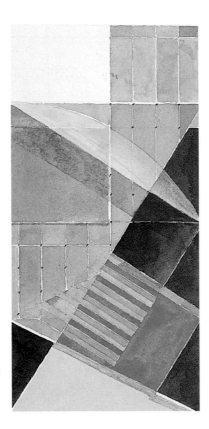

In designing for children, playground equipment was intentionally excluded due to its single use, overriding safety concerns, and studies that indicate its limited appeal to children. Mark Rios, a designer of children's play environments, argues that the prefabricated play apparatus "dictates a certain way to use it, which is climbing. But developing physical skills accounts for only 10 percent of all activity at the playground." [16] In Day Two, children are seen as adventurous, curious, and imaginative. Games are played on various surfaces: turf, sand, decomposed granite, asphalt, and concrete, and the children have access to various spaces. The sandbox is the only feature that is sacred: it is a place for the smaller tots to mold and make things under the watchful eyes of guardians. The play yard, with its diversity for play, learning, and new experiences, allows children to invent by creating connections between real objects and their environment.

The Playhouse

The two girls have a tea party on the plane of sloping grass. They pretend the playhouse/tool shed is their home. In the sandbox, two kids build a castle with tools borrowed from the gardeners. The two girls yell at their brothers who are busy playing a game something like tag, cops-and-robbers, and hide-and-seek all rolled into one. Their activities transform the whole scene into a playground.

Spring brings out the gazanias and the lovers. With their bumpers of Old E from the corner store, they sit at the picnic table, and maybe they don't even talk. They sit there together. They watch the street, together.

Lovers

The third transformation begins with a metaphorical construct, the lovers. The space becomes primarily a proscenium for human relationships to develop. A perch is proposed which looms high above the space. As a place for couples, friends, or the weary, it allows privacy away from the other activities at ground level.

This is a familiar place for those who want privacy but who also want to be seen. Fruit blossoms, sage, and a blue aura permeate the space. The perch is a simple construction: a balloon frame structure with a metal roof. Railings and stairs offer safety and access. The roof is a simple double gable. This is a place for encounters, conversations, and love.

The Perch

They come to sit together, whether at street level or in the tower rising above the neighborhood. Accentuating their isolation and solidarity, their intimacy becomes more powerful. Their coupleness is visible to the street. Looking out on the street. There to be seen. To have a space of their own, together, as long as this sunset lasts.

Day Four

Brown paper bags in hand, they leave

the store and head straight for the park.

It is the stopping point to drink a beer

and take in the sights along the street.

A picnic table and two benches are the

only seats. Once the beer is consumed,

they go on their way.

Beer Drinkers

Seen by many as an illicit act in the neighborhood, the consumption of alcoholic beverages on public grounds is prohibited. When I think of such prohibitions, my thoughts turn to the beautiful beer gardens of Europe and, even closer to home, to the occasional beer drunk by a suburbanite while sitting on the porch on a warm afternoon after mowing the lawn. In recent times, the sale of beer in the neighborhood is the number one economic resource to the neighborhood merchant. The popularity of the forty- and sixty-ounce malt liquor beer in marginal ethnic communities is a coup for distributors and corporations. More malt liquor for less money.

The beer garden is a simple programmatic response to a familiar neighborhood use: it is not a place for beer sales, but a space to sit and relax, where beer consumption is accepted, not prohibited. With its trimmed rows of trees, seating, garden cultivation, and shelter at the street-side, the space is welcoming to the beer drinker. The familiar in this case is not judged but incorporated.

Beer Garden

Rows of seats are filled on a hot day.

Bags in hand, they all share stories and a

laugh or two. Those who want to be seen

sit on the porch. Others sit towards the

back, lounging, watching the gardeners,

the lovers, and the children at play.

Day Five

I had to pull the car over to let them by. Carts banging against one another—the sound of glass is musical, like that of a chandelier near an open window. One guides from the front, the other pushes mechanically from the back. Like a train, the carts and their conductors plod down the center of the street. A choreographed dance, the one in the rear casually slips away, returning with prizes scooped from Gertrude's trash. Pulling and pushing, they continue down the center of the street, oblivious to the cars maneuvering around them.

I awake to a mysterious rattle and peer at the clock which reads 3:00 A.M. A distant rattle grows to a clang and then a beautiful chorus of tinkles. I turn over and resume my sleep—the chorus slips past. Bottles fill my dreams. In the morning, the bag of empty beer bottles I left at the door is gone.

Recycling

In the final layer of Day Five, all of the proposed needs are met. The cultivation and its accouterments expand along the eastern boundary. Sage and lavender borders lace the bottom of evergreen hedges that enclose the seating spaces. An allée of fruit trees marches along the western boundary. The sandbox is tucked between bamboo stands at the rear of the site. The perch is expanded to two rooms next to the street. The final programmatic piece is a recycling structure. It is wide enough for shopping carts to roll through. This construction allows residents to bring their recycling materials to the park, and those who collect along the street can now come and retrieve items on a daily basis. This concept is antithetical to the city's program, which denies collection to the cart people. The recycling use forces the architectural "lump" to expand in meaning and use: a utility room, a recycling shed, and whatever is imaginable by children.

Set together in a beautiful composition, the perch, the multiuse structure, the garden, sandbox, seating, and flora, transform the space into a unique and particular place. No single programmatic piece dominates the space—the ethic of difference and inclusion creates a place with multiple meanings—one that underscores many neighborhood issues at odds with normative societal values and attitudes.

Recycling Bins

They are always there first thing in the morning to clean out the bright yellow recycling bins. I left mine there last night, a small bucket of bottles. As if they were shopping in a grocery store, they steer the carts down the aisles, sorting bottles and cans to take to the recycling center. Other collectors come too late. The recycling shed has been cleared. I return after work to get my bucket.

Durant Minipark, Day One: The Garden

Durant Minipark, Day Three: The Perch

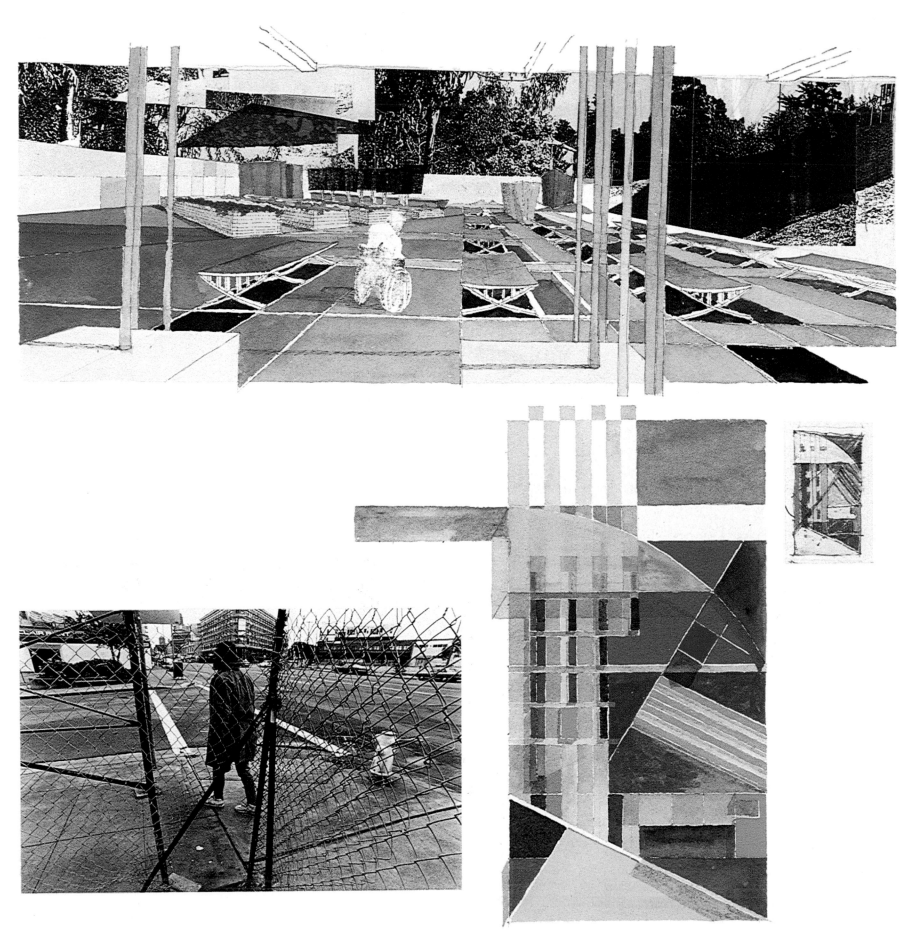

Durant Minipark, Day Four: Beer Garden

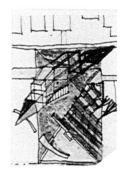

Durant Minipark, Day Five: Recycling Bins

25th Street Park—
The Corner Park

Purchased in 1976, the corner park's site was once occupied by commercial and residential buildings. It is located at the intersection of a major commercial street/residential arterial (four lanes) and a residential street (two lanes). It exhibits standard features typical of parks built in the 1970s: hardy trees (eucalyptus), game tables, benches, and manufactured play equipment. A large, amorphously shaped sandbox is equipped with the various play apparatuses. A small seating area is placed at the corner and buffered from the street by shrubs and trees. The park makes little attempt to embrace the public corner and the major arterial, Martin Luther King Jr. Way, that passes by.

The space is now primarily a place for a transient group of elderly men. Some disabled, some retired, and others unemployed, they while away the mornings and afternoons on the corner benches that face into the park. On some days a song can be heard coming from behind the seat wall, or, with bags of 40s in hand, they sit and tell stories and lies about past and current events. Every once in a while a child can be observed in the cold and shadowed sandbox playing on the playground apparatuses. Racketeering is common as a part of the leisure day at the park. At night the grounds lie fallow, unlit and unfit for the homeless to find a place of refuge out of sight of the passersby.

The planned framework for design transformation is a set of simple geometries: circle, square, and triangle. The diagram is free of any preconceived programs, open to interpretation.

25th Street Park

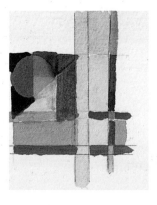

They are there all day—the shuck/jiving flows like liquid from the mouths of the old. Their faces show signs of time-aged copper; each line bears a story, a tale, an adventure. The wheelchair man moves back and forth from store to corner. The bag man is always at the bench playing cards. The young hustlers try to play, but it's the storytellers who have lived: they've heard the angels.

Performers

I remember puppet shows: Punch and Judy in the park and at streetside as a small boy in Fontainebleau, France. Years later my grandfather would sit on his porch and tell his grandkids stories about his youth and his kids (our parents), along with other impressive tales and adventures meant for excited kids. During my adolescence, the local park always featured the old guy seated with a crowd around him, telling heroic tales from his life. Or time was passed listening to and watching the big guys (eighteen-year-olds) on the corner, on the steps of the popular family's house, or on the basketball court and around the picnic tables. They were telling us how to be men! These were all great performances.

Improvisational theater is a cultural norm, free for all who will lend an ear. Can you imagine a city without theater, a place where histories or myths cannot be heard?

Theater

A stage awaits the storytellers; they come from all over; strong like the oak, they share their knowledge, firmly rooted in time. They linger on the street and lawn just to reminisce about the good ol' days and their bad ol' ways.

The theaters unfold from the framework at the park's inside and outside corners: one is round, one rectilinear, and the other triangular. They provide for a nonobjective assembly awaiting human transfiguration.

The round theater occupies the inside corner of the park. Turf creates a thick green carpet underfoot, slightly "crowned" at its apex to give optical and physical emphasis to its center. A steel-edge header marks the circumference. Near the circle, a triangular planting bed reinforces the outer edge. Composed of French lavender or red twig dogwoods, the plants enclose the green circular floor. Tall Lombardy poplars are planted along the circle's circumference, projecting upward, creating a slender green proscenium.

The rectilinear amphitheater is split, with a gravel path connecting the three theaters. Constructed with poured-in-place concrete, every other tread is sown with turf. A wood platform sealed with anodized coloring is underfoot for the performers. Viewers can look forward or sideways depending on which performance they choose to view. The last theater is simply a rectilinear allée, graced with flowering crab apples planted in an eighteen-foot-wide, decomposed granite walkway. People mingle here as the actors, musicians, and storytellers traverse its path. Cars pass or stop to partake in the streetside events.

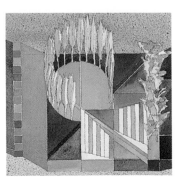

Day Two

Sometimes I think that an accident has happened or a block party is on, but it is just a good day. Ten to fifteen people just relaxing, strolling, leaning, sitting–chillin' out. Nowhere to go, nothing to do. Time on their hands.

Chillin'

Everyday I pass, they are there on the corner. Every age and sex, kids, young adults, and the old and fragile. The doors of houses are wide open, and household chairs occupy the sidewalk. Across the street in the park, older gentlemen sit, waving and talking, just shooting the breeze. Cars stop mid-block with their music blaring out, filling the air of the socially vibrant but physically bleak landscape.

Shelters and Chairs

In chairs, under trees, out at the curb, or the grassy steps, the corner park is full. She is telling a story about the fire last week. A dice game starts under the shelter. Each corner is occupied. Cars go by slowly, looking for familiar faces.

The park accommodates two new shelters and a multitude of new chairs. The theater is reoriented toward both streets. Half of its seats are turf, and the other half are concrete. The shelters are multi-dimensional, serving as protection from the elements, orientation, access, and space-makers. One is long and linear, marking a formal entry to the circular amphitheater. The other is wed to the red stage at the corner. Each is made of steel, with narrow vertical supports. One floats above the corner, providing a ceiling, and the other presents a gable roof, directing you into the space. The chairs are fabricated with wood and steel as they are in a French park: beautiful chairs for beautiful people.

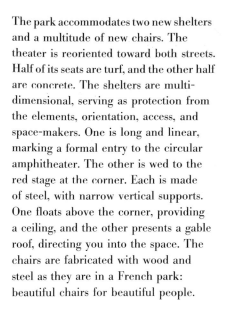

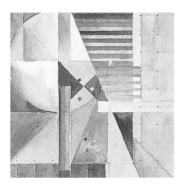

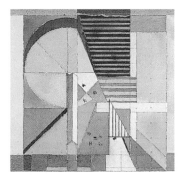

Standing there with two ropes, they are waiting for her to start double dutch. The housing project's driveway is small and hard, but it is their only play area. One tree struggles alone at the street, half-dead from neglect and abuse.

Play Yard

Children are amazingly creative when time is at a premium. On a hot day, an opened hydrant creates a lap pool in the street's concrete gutter. A complete baseball diamond can be imagined along the six-foot-wide sidewalk. Amazingly, the ball always stays in bounds. A basketball hoop (milk crate) gets nailed to a Pacific Gas & Electric pole, and the "Berkeley Farms Dairy" basketball league begins its long season. Timberform, Pipeline, and Big Toys can learn a lot from these improvised acts. No safety surface! Skinned knees and elbows are wounds of an adventurous and exciting day. Years later the scars are reminders of our youth, a time when risk and abandonment are permissible.

Day Three at the park produces a tripartite park program. The theater, chillin' areas, and children's play yard are commingled along meandering paths, with colorful asphalt block and concrete paving. The theater is central to all activities. The shelter becomes a simple trellis which leads into a newly planted eucalyptus wood. Fast growing, aromatic, and wild, the wood is a primeval environment. A tree house and bridge trace through the treetops, mitigating the youngsters' yells and frolic. Two tree houses are built, one red and the other yellow, anchoring the steel tension bridge. The red tree house roof is open to the trees, while the yellow one is closed with four metal pitched roofs: an altar to the woods. It is not easy to negotiate entry to the houses and bridge. Only the agile and adventurous can make the climb up into the treetops.

Tree House

The girls jump rope and dance at the corner where a crowd has gathered; it is always more fun with an audience. The wheelchair man is talking but takes a moment to yell to the boys up in the eucalyptus woods to be a little quiet. They cannot hear him: the trees buffer them from his reprimand. They run along the bridge laughing and playing.

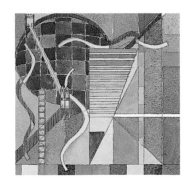

Day Four

Every evening the steel drum blazes with

fire. Tonight they have hot dogs. Emerging

from behind the timber and canvas hut,

he zips his trousers and continues drinking.

She makes food for all of them. The meat

changes daily, depending on what they've

collected.

Barbecuing

The city prohibits barbecuing in urban public open spaces. If you travel to regional, state, and national parks, you'll discover picnic areas with smoking barbecues and camp fires. Allowable in landscapes that were once pristine forests, chaparral preserves, and redwood forests, fire is not allowed in the hard urban landscape. Why is it that the people who live in the city aren't trusted? Fire is primal for warmth, cooking, and ambient and focal glow. The steel drum has outgrown the backyard barbecue in these parts; on its side or stood on end, a blaze can be set and the smoking started.

Day Four is a time to feast. The hybrid scenario is reminiscent of midtwentieth-century America's Fourth of July feasts in town squares and parks, or the fish fry common throughout African American neighborhoods nationwide. Two sixteen-foot-long, sturdy, wood-plank tables grace the park's corner, anchored by a red concrete-block hearth with two surface grills and a central oven. The craft of each reflects a desire for quality. A new rest room facility provides sanitation, relief, and storage. The accouterments belong to the park, a return to the California modernist dream of outdoor living.

Dinner

She sets the table today. A long white

table cloth and fresh bread. She reminds

them all to wash up—tonight is special.

The fire is hot, and the chicken sets it

ablaze. They all gather round to listen to

tales and laughter, drinking and waiting

for dinner.

Day Five

Asleep on the street—behind bushes,

walking through the night—

I don't know them but they look familiar.

My people. My people.

My studio has heat, a toilet, a bed.

Why do I question my "have," comparing

it to their "have nots." Guilt, pity, shame,

innocence, all at once. They are human

like us. Why are they here?

My people. My people.

Homeless

I've noticed two cars parked along the street, a truck and a sedan. They are both occupied all day and night—everyday! In the truck sits a white male. His face is scruffy and unshaven. The truck is filled with old papers, magazines, and other printed matter. He sits in the driver's seat with his head down, reading in the quiet solace of his cab. A half block down the street is the sedan. Blankets, bags of clothing, and other household items fight for space on the car seats and dash board. The car also reveals a young African American couple and their small baby. The father in the front, the mother and child in the back. A few weeks ago they disappeared. Rumor has it that a neighbor complained to the police. The white guy in the truck is still there. Words like "homeless," "houseless," "vagrant," "transient," "bum" all signify those without shelter. They are a commonplace sight in the American urban environment. Whether sleeping in cars, parks, or on the street, they call the public landscape home.

Housing

A row of father-son-holy-ghost dwellings

infills the block. Each has a yard, a picket

fence, and a front stoop. They watch over

the corner and participate in storytelling.

The lawn and promenade give the street

to neighbors, grilling, playing, strolling,

getting to know one another.

All are welcome on Day Five in the park. The activities from the previous days are all accommodated. Row housing is built along the 25th Street edge of the park. They call them father-son-holy-ghost houses or a bandbox type, ". . .developed on the interior blocks of Philadelphia on lots sized 13 feet by 20 feet. This building type dates from circa 1750. Each building has one room per floor and is three or four floors high." [17] The row houses provide minimum living requirements. Seven three-story units amount to 1820 square feet of park space, or one twenty-fifth of an acre. This is a small sacrifice of open space in return for a greater good: housing for people. Each house has a small stoop at streetside and a small rear yard adjacent to the park.

Features from previous days: the theater, chillin' chairs and shelters, children's play areas, the hearth and dining area, and rest room facilities greet the new families and neighbors. Now there is a place with permanent residents who watch over the park while patrons, young and old, partake in the daily acts of living in the city.

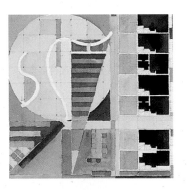

25th Street Park, Day Five: Proscenium Model

25th Street Park, Day Two: Chairs and Shelter

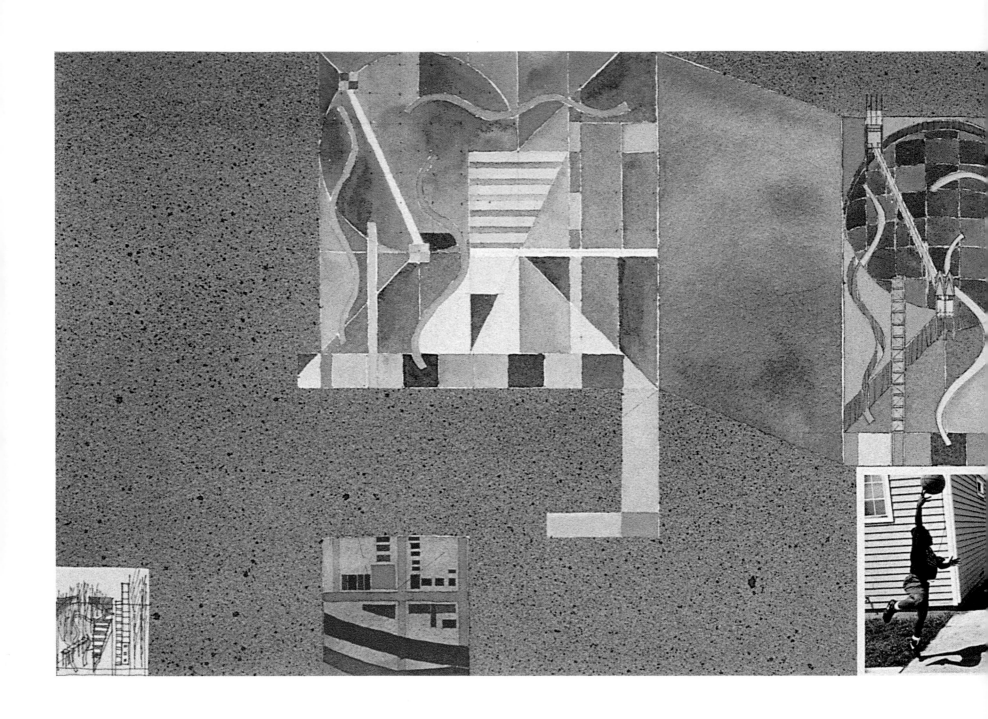

25th Street Park, Day Three: Tree House

Grove Shafter Park–
The Freeway Park

The landscape of Grove Shafter Park was once a mixed-use residential and commercial corridor. Then in 1969 the freeway came. The Department of Housing and Urban Development, local officials, and neighborhood advocates decided that the space within the freeway right-of-way should become a neighborhood park, a model idea at the time, and purchased it in 1976-78.

Located beneath the MacArthur Freeway and I-980 interchange, Grove Shafter Park is five and one-half acres in size, segmented into three parts by freeway ramps, streets, and overpasses. Compared to other sites, the park's program is more diverse. Sited within its picturesque green landscape are basketball courts, manufactured play equipment, rest room facilities (abandoned), benches, game tables, and eucalyptus trees.

The freeway interchange is a vast geometric field. Elevated cars and trucks hurl by, as if they were in a scene from the film *Metropolis*. Below the massive freeway ramps, a bucolic landscape lies fallow. The majority of human activity occurs at the park's edges, while, in the adjacent streets, a few commercial entities and homes stand in reverence to the freeway. The freeway is a modern-day engineering feat. Rationally designed, a nine-square grid completes the system for throughways, ramps, and merge lanes. Bisecting the freeway along its north-south axis, the Bay Area Rapid Transit trains run beneath, separating north- and southbound lanes. In a piecemeal fashion, the park occupies only three of the freeway's quadrants.

Today there are usually more people in front of the liquor store adjacent to the park than in the park itself. The picturesque spaces beneath the freeway seem surreal as cars swoosh by overhead, beside, and below. A machine landscape of movement, light, and sound holds the visitor's senses captive. Transients find refuge here, where they can drink and engage in other types of illicit activities in the vast freeway landscape. Proclaimed innovative when initially conceived, the park now lies fallow. The proposed framework for design is derived from the intersecting freeway's basic geometry: four squares define where roads and ramps extend and intersect in four directions.

Grove Shafter Park

Day One

They dress in black. Raiders jackets
nostalgic for Oakland's football legacy.
Five or six at a time, hanging out in front
of one of the many "grocery stores"
(a.k.a. liquor stores) on MLK Way.
A colorless field of images—lethargic
and gaunt—a shadow of self. Territorial
gestures and acts of distrust, warring
signs as forms of communication. Zora
Neale Hurston's resigned words, "my
people, my people," echo in my mind.
Solutions seem large, too large to grasp.
Will they work, or is it too late?

Industry

There is an abundance of youth spending the majority of their time in the streets. Their numbers have swelled as opportunities for work and play have diminished. Speaking recently with a young African American male at a park workshop, I was inspired by the breadth of his understanding of the predicament that many like him face in the twentieth-century city. Looking for ways to participate in the rebuilding of his community, he spoke with confidence and sincerity about the decline of his local park and the way his age group had recently been neglected in park programming and planning. He spoke of the lack of male figures to guide him. He spoke of the creativity that the staff needed to overcome their fears and biases toward his generation. He spoke of simple remedies to what others see as large problems. He spoke of creating new opportunities. Put simply, he spoke out.

Day One proposes introducing industry as a new program. Car shops, actually rental spaces for commerce in parking lots, are built against the freeway ramps in long, narrow strips. Their widths are derived from the automobile: the same as auto-parking stalls, with maximum dimensions of twelve feet by twenty feet. Simple, four-story building structures on pilotis provide parking on the ground floor, shops on the second and third floors, and living space or storage on the fourth floor. The domino-like frames are constructed of concrete with wood-frame construction infilled, sheathed, and painted. The second floor has a tilted-out steel screen for security and promotional

signage. You can buy or lease one, two, or as many spaces as suit your needs. Some shops are spaced in alternating fashion, featuring deck space between buildings. As a result of siting the car shops against the freeway ramps, large rectilinear and square open spaces remain, providing opportunities for an urban wood, a large circular playing field, and a sloping grassy plane for kite flying and ramp watching. An expansive edge of sweet gum trees are planted, forming a thick line at the depressed freeway edge. Local residents, as well as outsiders coming off the freeway, frequent the car shops.

Work Shops

Cars fill the stalls before 9:00 A.M.
Car shops offer start-up space to any
neighborhood business, from barber to
bookshop, seamstress to shoe repair.
The guys are trying their luck at selling
silk-screened T-shirts, their own artwork
displayed on their chests. Their signs
tilt out. By 9:30 A.M., all are open for
business.

Day Two

He lives under the underpass. I see him in the throes of his incantations as I drive past. A strong build of a man, a god or monk who watches over the surreal highway landscape. His magic is kept hidden within the dense freeway planting. When he needs to perform ritual, he sets up on the basketball court.

Housing

To clear away an area for the construction of the MacArthur Freeway and I-980, three or four city blocks of housing and commercial or institutional establishments were removed. To replace the lost residential dwellings, subsidized, multifamily complexes were built on isolated city blocks or infilled between vacated or fallow residential lots. Seen as a remedy for the decay of the older urban fabric, a new, modern environment was imagined. In the spirit of modernism, planners and designers envisioned a fresh start.

Today, as you traverse the Grove Shafter Park site, it is easy to imagine where those "blighted" structures sat. On the fringe, homes that were not in the way are still inhabited. The irony in the superimposition of the freeway structure and its partners, redevelopment and modernism, is that the clean slate that was created through subtraction has become a clogged machine. Travelers are transported through a landscape that never became clean, but is once again considered dirty from the machines that traverse it. The gigantic scale of the freeway will never come down to the ground to serve the community. But can the community rise up and beyond the limitations that the freeway imposes?

The new program adds housing to the industrial enterprises below the freeway and has to reckon with the maze of freeway structures. Placed at the major intersection of Martin Luther King Jr. Way and 34th Street, the new housing is a series of four towers and a long rectilinear building that stretches across the freeway. The four towers are reminiscent of Leon Krier's proposal for St. Peter's Square at the junction of the Via Condotta and Via Corso in Rome. He proposed both urban monuments and social centers to replace the decadent institutions of church and state, the cathedrals and schools. The proposed towers in West Oakland are a new social

center, with housing as a primary use. Head Start, daycare, and nursery school are provided on the upper floors, along with a community center and a health facility. The new elements are elevated high above the freeway landscape, offering young and old visual access to the world outside the freeway ramps. The housing that stretches across the freeway is actually built on a bridge, reconnecting West Oakland with its eastern neighbors. Augmenting the bridge/houses are the car industries from Day One and the new open spaces, which mitigate the vision of the freeway from the ground. The fourth quadrant of the freeway's geometry is wiped clean, awaiting change in days to come.

Housing

Standing at the apex of the pyramid, habitual staff in hand, he presides over the newly built housing complexes. People living here seek him out for advice. He is the neighborhood magician now. His magic has served him well.

Day Three

When the sun comes out on MLK Way,
people emerge from the shadows of
houses, apartment complexes, storefronts,
and vacant lots. Animated by light, the
street and sidewalk display movement.
Blackness of light and skin—quick
movements and crowds. The ball court
is alive with the loud clanging of a hoop
missing its net. The laughter of kids
running and playing on the sidewalk.

Recreation

The redevelopment campaign of the late 1960s and 1970s in West Oakland, as in other American cities, proclaimed that the lack of recreational facilities and open space were contributing causes of the community's demise. Social and recreational programs and facilities were created to provide improvement for the neighborhood youth and elderly population. As remedies for the array of problems that plagued the neighborhood, they offered alternatives and respite from the harsh environment. Many, like myself, whose adolescent experiences are a product of this era, wonder why these programs and facilities are no longer available. In Austin Allen's documentary film, *Claiming Open Space*, a retired park coordinator and dancer reminisces about the great programs and facilities Defermery Park offered in West Oakland. Organized dance programs, crafts, young men's group, dances, and so forth, created alternatives for play, education, and socialization in the neighborhood. Everyone in the neighborhood participated. It was a place of pride and hope.

As funds dwindled, however, staff and programs were cut and abandoned. Today the remaining community centers and parks operate with insufficient funding. Demographics have changed as new households grow younger and more residents rely on public assistance. The redevelopment programs and assistance were devised as temporary relief to enable residents to rise out of the subsidized existence. Many residents have been here since the bulldozers came, twenty-five to thirty years ago. A dependent culture has arisen out of these circumstances.

Community Center

Day Three proposes a new recreational and community center which spans the 34th Street bridge across the freeway and rapid transit course. The new center pierces ramps and merging lanes, towering above the spaghetti ramps filled with automobiles. The premise for this insertion is to create a metaphorical "bandage," healing a scar. The community center is a place to heal and return health and hope to the inhabitants.

The center is golden in color. A steel-frame structure with thin-cut marble inlays composes its facade. The new building catches light and shadow as it spans the scar of the freeway. The fourth quadrant, which was wiped clean in the previous day, is built upon in Day Three. A recycling center occupies this zone. The large building opens to a central storage yard. The building's scale is large. A collection of simple, tilted-up structures nudges up against the freeway ramps.

North of the new recreation center along Martin Luther King Jr. Way, adjacent to the new housing, a blues club is built for nighttime entertainment. Situated across the street from Eli's Mile High Club, an established music spot, the new club occupies the freeway quadrant. Court activities, like basketball, tennis, and handball, are provided between the blues club and the housing. The car shops occupy the quadrant at the corner of 34th Street, set amidst a grove of hardwood trees with a central green.

Community Center

Working with the kids at the center,
the recreation trainer realizes that, in
bridging the freeway, the center also
bridges the gap between two communities.
Kids and parents, east and west of I-980,
play and socialize at the new facility.
As she looks out the translucent window
toward Oakland's skyline, she senses a
completeness to her neighborhood.

Day Four

Every Sunday morning they leave the house. Dressed in their Sunday best, the two little girls are always late. Shining from Royal Crown, they come out running and racing for the coveted special place in the car. Mom is there waiting to give a quick lecture before departure. The sky is a wash of fog and baby blue. Sundays always feel like Sundays. The car turns the corner as the two shining faces peer from the rear window.

Religion

The area between Martin Luther King Jr. Way and Telegraph Avenue, where the freeway creates its rigid line, was once a landscape dotted with institutional structures. Every other block hosted a church. In the African American community the church has historically played a major role in shaping the community's world view and spirit. "Of all the institutions created by black Oaklanders in the nineteenth century, the church was the most important. In the 1890s, however, the increasing size and diversity of the black community created both the possibility and the need for a greater variety for religious expression." [18] These opportunities were manifested in the blocks of West Oakland but were later dismantled by the modern infrastructure.

Churches now inhabit structures vacated by businesses, old storefronts, warehouses, and apartment buildings. No longer set alone in the urban fabric, they now blend into the dilapidated streetscape of West Oakland. On Sundays the spirit can be heard on the street.

The new church binds a relationship between the sky and the ground. Situated in the quadrant north of the interchange, it is composed of two parallel buildings held high off the ground by a structural field of columns. Constructed of concrete, the church emulates its surroundings, hosting its own pedestrian ramps which ascend into its vacuous shell. One building holds classrooms, kitchens, a youth hostel, and other ancillary church functions. The other is the place for pews and the pulpit. Next to the church is the cemetery, which is composed of square cube structures. Each square plot begins sixty feet below the ground. Burial occurs in a vertical manner, with plots stacked on top of one another. Over time the squares will rise above the freeway, creating a city of the dead next to a house of worship for the living.

The Church

Once at church, the little girls race through the maze of headstones to join the other kids under the church for a game of tag. Elders walk up the ramp into the nave. Latecomers and children look up to the altar through the window to see pews quickly filling and the preacher approaching the altar.

All hurry in to join the service.

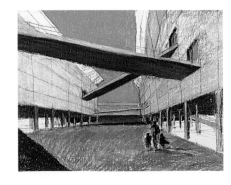

Day Five
The sidewalk is a stage for every imaginable act. Tables and chairs, barbecue grills, and sofas provide the accouterments.

Neighborhood

Landscape architect Randolph Hester suggests that neighborhoods are defined by their residents, not by their planners, and the definitions are expressed in the political actions taken by residents. [19] He further suggests that neighborhoods embody "collective responsibility," which arises from people's shared values, use patterns, and common problems. The characteristics that Hester identifies are important in defining and understanding communities, and indicate residents' awareness that they are in the same boat together. Many urban neighborhoods are homogeneous and even exclusive, unless adventurous (artist) or transient (student) populations commingle. The situation has left marginally economic neighborhoods isolated, separated by class, race, and economic and political orientation. A neighborhood should embody diversity, but not at the expense of economic vitality. West Oakland is a living testament to Hester's vision of a neighborhood, in that it is a community where similar values, attitudes, and patterns of use are shared. The political and collective responsibilities, however, are not present. With the low economic status, fractious physical conditions, and environmental injustices associated with the imposed freeways, mail station, BART, and so forth, inhabitants have grown apathetic about the possibility of political change.

The final layer at the Grove Shafter Park produces a melodic complex of community components. Establishing themselves physically within the confines of the freeway's nine-square geometry, design components depart from the one-dimensional artifact. Day Five brings a multidimensional development to the new neighborhood, redressing thirty years of subtractive forces. The four new quadrants of the freeway landscape act in unison, reconnecting the freeway's mammoth split and encouraging resident participation at the site.

Describing the development in a clockwise fashion, beginning at the top right, the first quadrant is a landscape for recreational opportunities. Outdoor court areas and a large grass playing field are joined to the eastern end of the new recreational and community center by a blue bridge structure stretching across the freeway at 34th Street. The bridge accommodates two bridge buildings, one at each side of the road. The smaller one houses commercial shops paralleling the recreation center's armature. Both are appendages of activity and commerce. The commercial complex merges with Martin Luther King Jr. Way, displaying a corner plaza and a shady bosk and outdoor market area. The recreation center features a gymnasium, weight room, showers, daycare, classrooms, game rooms, offices, and a health center. As the structure reaches Martin Luther King Jr. Way, it is joined together with two middle- and low-income rental and condominium housing towers. Community facilities are located in the upper floors. Behind this complex the second quadrant features a grove of hardwood trees. The breadth of the grove creates a dark and mysterious urban wood, encapsulating the car shops which rise between the freeway ramps.

The third quadrant features a multi-denomination church. Its spaces can be rented seven days a week by any congregation in the community. Two white buildings back up against the freeway, presenting a sacred face to the street. Three large triangles compose its inward-facing landscape. Two are heavily planted with Mexican sage, and the center triangle is a grassy incline. The concrete church towers above the ground, its inner, open courtyard a refuge for pedestrian ramps and sky. Directly adjacent to the church is a new blues and jazz club. The sacred and the profane are united, a constant reminder of their duality in our lives.

The fourth quadrant is a neighborhood recycling center. Here shopping carts, trucks, and cars full of recyclable cans are deposited. Instead of city-sponsored recycling pickups, new jobs are created by turning this service over to neighborhoods. A new pedestrian bridge connects the recycling center to the west side of the freeway, with its armature sliding between the church and the freeway. The recycling center is masked by a green wall composed of gabions planted with vines and shrubs. The wall separates the collection yard and building from the freeway ramps that slice through and above it.

The MacArthur Freeway and I-980 interchange is still a physical presence on Day Five, but the neighborhood has risen above it.

Community

Walking down Martin Luther King Jr. Way, the activities from the buildings and recreation areas permeate into the street. Everything works together: street-life, reclaimed open space, and new interventions. The diverse uses are in conversation with one another. The marketplace's color and aroma complement the neighborhood car shops. The forest, cemetery, and blues club create a diverse environment for exploration.

Grove Shafter Park, Day One: Work Shops

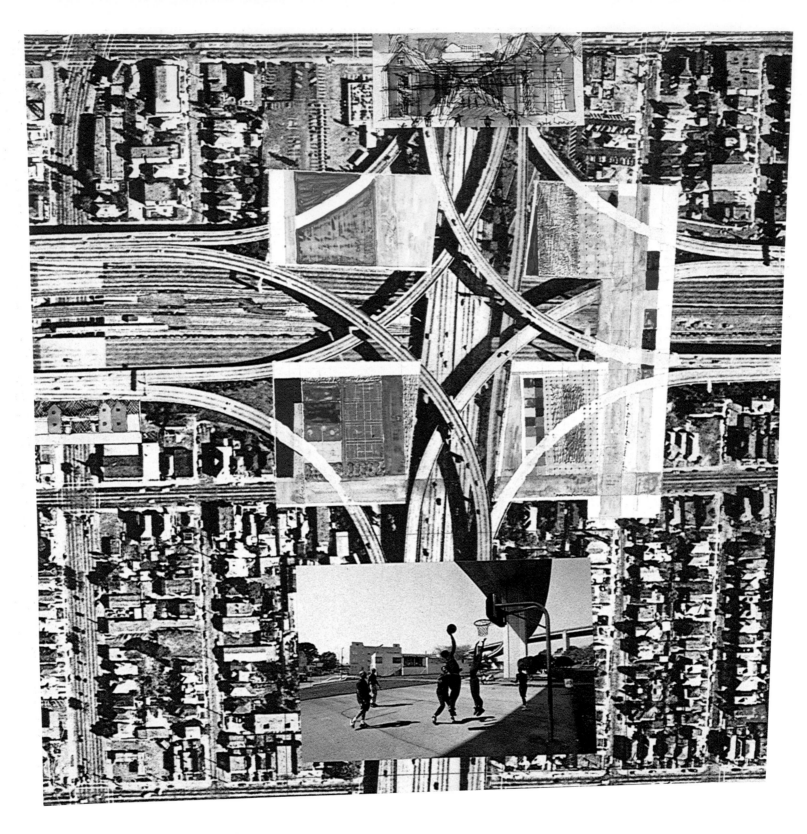

Grove Shafter Park, Day Three: Community Center

Grove Shafter Park, Day Five: Community

The Street

As the research unfolds, it becomes clear that the streets around the parks are more often used as open space than the parks themselves. As the pulse of activity, the streets also become a part of the diaries. As Jane Jacobs said, "The more successfully a city mingles everyday diversity of uses and users in its everyday streets, the more successfully, casually (and economically) its people thereby enliven and support well located parks that can thus give back grace and delight to their neighborhoods instead of vacuity." [20]

Commingling design interventions between the parks and the streets responds to the life and times of the neighborhood. The mixture responds to the total environment, creating a diversity of interpretations and uses of public space. 29th Street and Martin Luther King Jr. Way are the two streets that support these parks. Human action and need are investigated, producing site-specific improvisations that support the mundane patterns and practices of everyday life.

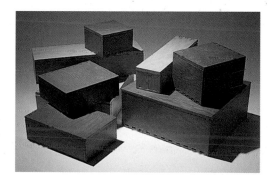

Day One

Simultaneous images of Oprah project out

onto the street from three color TV

consoles. Two tables, a recliner, and a

broken lamp complete the living room

ensemble on the lawn. A tall brother is

drinking a bumper of Old E as two big

guys unload a set of yard chairs from

the truck. As Oprah goes to a commercial

break, Johnny Gill kicks in from the

stereo lodged in the upstairs window.

Two cut girls emerge onto the street,

bustin' a few new moves. Three naval

cadets stop to purchase a chair. The scene

is quite surreal: Johnny Gill and the feet

and hands of the two girls, buyers and

sellers take over the street.

29th Street

The Transfigured Driveway

The driveway is placed at the edge of the single-family, open-lot plan. It extends from the street to the back of the house. Historically it may have connected a rear garage or carriage house to the street, but today it leads to a concrete patio. The driveways are concrete floors derived from automobile measurements, usually ten to fifteen feet wide.

On 29th Street, cars are stacked in the driveway, or they are parked along the street front for a quicker and easier exit. In the latter case the driveways become places for auto repair, car washing, children's games, the depositing of collectible goods, or the repair of an occasional boat.

The driveway already hosts many activities, from birthday parties to basketball games. The selling booth establishes itself inside this scene, transforming the driveway to host another form of activity. The residents of the house on 29th Street need a place to protect, display, and sell their collections. They will no longer have to cart them on and off the truck for display on the lawn. Now they will have a proscenium for all to see.

The selling block is composed of five major pieces: roof, floor, columns, wall, and ramp. Classically ordered, they compose a side porch to the yard's front. The blue wall is the block's signature, a stained stucco armature—firm, thick, and scaleless, a tribute to the image of artist David Hockney's California. The wall and driveway are "environmental fortuna." [21] Once constructed along the property line, the wall is simply a fence between neighbors: with the addition of a floor, roof, and columns, storage opportunities unfold. The roof is constructed of brushed metal, reflecting the sky and protecting the collectibles below. Connected to the wall and the columns, the roof sheds water across the front and into a scupper on the wall side. The runoff will fall flush, sheeting down the front side and, once atop the wall, gush down along a forty-five degree angle "scar" into a drain at ground level. Six columns march across the front, tall and slender, pushing the roof upward. Centrally located at the selling block's front, the ramp slips between two columns connecting the yard's central sidewalk. The selling block is raised onto a concrete dock for easy loading and unloading.

Sitting tall and proud, the selling block has now replaced the driveway. The collectors have a place of business, keeping their collections dry, protected, and in full view of the street.

The Selling Block

With items neatly displayed against the

wall, the stage is set for today's sales. The

bargaining and dealing are ready to com-

mence. The first on the block: two color

TV's and a Thonet chair. The truck backs

up to the dock and unloads a brass bed.

A customer rushes over to make her bid.

29th Street, Day One: The Selling Block

Day Two

Razor-sharp shadows cut across the asphalt as the sun sets down 29th Street. Baby is shonuff strutting as boys and men rubberneck in her direction. Looking up and down the street she adjusts the slit of her skirt to reveal a long white leg. Within minutes a midnight blue Blazer cautiously motions by. Baby nods to the driver, all the while scanning the streets for detection. With a simple gesture, he befriends her, and she hops into the waiting door. The journey is a short two hundred feet. The "date" itself is very quick—two or three minutes. He makes a sharp U-turn and drops her off at the place of origin. As she saunters back down the street, he takes one final look before driving away.

Street Walkers' Drive-In

In the pages of Anaïs Nin and Henry Miller, promiscuity, lust, and money are the daily realities of the street. The pattern of street prostitution is closely associated with neighborhood blight, in real life as in literature. Selection of the right neighborhood, intersection, and street is of central importance to the prostitute: most preferred are neighborhoods where apathy is high and police surveillance scarce. Amongst dilapidated buildings, liquor stores, and apartment complexes, the women of the street solicit all who pass their way. The act of prostitution typically takes place within the confines of the visitor's automobile. Once a selection is made, the couple chooses a private place to park for the performance of services. Under the freeway, curbside next to vacant buildings, the automobile is the only buffer between the sex act and an audience of neighbors. In full view to passing children or an occasional glance from a nearby window, the auto and its actors seem to be cloaked in invisibility.

In many major cities, "red light" districts are established to house the dark sides of our desires, featuring institutions that cater to the needs of the lonely. Prostitution, long illegalized in most states, is nevertheless present in a blaze of lights and beautiful women.

The drive-through brothel is a new institution to the neighborhood street. It shrouds the prostitute and the partner and thus makes them visible in the community. The drive-in brothel's dimensions are familiar, governed by the shape and size of the automobile. Like a parking space, it takes up residence at curbside. The roof and doors are the union of two circles, representing male and female. The lower circle is retractable and the upper is stationary. Once the car enters, a door lowers itself along an inside track. Coin and dollar bill operated, particular amounts are deposited for various time settings: five, ten, or fifteen minutes. Vending machines are featured on the inside, stocked with contraceptives.

Drive-In Brothel
She accepts his nod and jumps in the front seat of the car. He is middle-aged and white; she is tall and black. They drive slowly as she discusses payment. Once at the booth, the car disappears. She drops in the tokens and the doors come down. Fifteen minutes later, he is satisfied, and she is a little richer.

The Street Stadium

The American urban residential street is an extension of the gridiron plan from the city center. Prior to the establishment of the automobile, American streets sheltered a diversity of social patterns: places to meet and walk, grounds for vendors and merchants, and space for children's games. Neighborhoods were synonymous with the streets that traversed them. As traffic from automobiles proliferated, neighborhood streets became places that have excluded the human.

During the late 1960s, American sentiment returned to the social uses of the street in the context of the closed-street mall. By eliminating automobile traffic to the central core of the downtown, social life could return. The first, Fresno Street Mall in Fresno, California, closed its borders to the car, allowing merchants and residents a free environment. Many cities followed suit. Eventually the closed-street mall grew to accommodate transit, improving the availability of parking and shortening walking distances from transit to the mall.

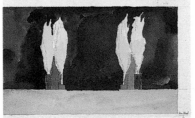

The new, vehicle-free streets, however, were plagued by a central problem: how to foster a broad, continuous cycle of life. Once the automobile was eliminated, events and social activity only occurred in relationship to the businesses that operated in the area.

The closed and slow street has seduced many residential neighborhoods as well. Contemporary neighborhoods propose speed bumps or humps to slow the automobile and deter traffic. It's an ongoing battle by public officials and residents to reconcile the automobile and the street.

A vibrant street life is produced by the mixture of diverse events and variables. Street football games played by children or the New York City street stick ball made famous by nostalgic stories did not occur because of Woonerfs, bumps, humps, barriers, or street closure. Streets functioning as playgrounds are a reality in working-class neighborhoods, and they present a picture that is quite different from the Norman Rockwell-like idea of the American neighborhood street.

Donald Appleyard's "seven points" [22] for the ideal street offer ideas to help reclaim and improve the quality of street life. But he leaves one issue unresolved: the inclusion of automobiles and the socialization that takes place in and around them. Cars are a familiar and essential part of the American cultural scene. In working-class neighborhoods, the car is often an indicator of social

status. For many, it's the only piece of capital investment and therefore takes center stage to daily activities. Stopping and starting, newsing, tinkering creates congregation in the neighborhood quarter. Cultural geographer Paul Groth, in his essay on vernacular parks, advocates plurality of uses to include traditional patterns. He makes the analogy between a shelter for picnic tables and a shelter for car waxing. [23] Following this same theme, uses along the street should include the familiar patterns that accompany humans and their automobiles.

29th Street is a two-lane street with parking at both curbs. Single-family residential lots, multifamily units, and institutional and light industrial uses are commingled along its edges. The stadium is created by simple architectural gestures: the placement of stoop benches along the side of the street, planting tall poplar trees at regular spaces between the benches, and draining the street across its crown, employing French drains placed every ten yards.

Cars are still allowed on the street, although the drains slow the traffic. People gather to sit at the benches beneath the shadow of the poplars as the game begins. When there is no game, cars can park next to the stoop benches. With doors open and music aloud, streetside becomes an extension of the car. Gatherings, waxing the car, and other social opportunities unfold.

Street Stadium

Moments after the big game, the residents of the streets take their seats to participate in their own game. Tall poplars shimmer like banners above a stadium as the game gets into gear and the street is alive with cheering.

Day Four

She seems lost, prancing back and forth,
up and down the street. Dark shadows
hide her face—bitter eyes dance, subservient
due to need. Like magic, her appearance
is quick. In a flash she has made a
decision: she heads towards that familiar
car. Appearing and disappearing.

A Home

The lack of affordable housing in America has reached epidemic proportions today. Even more, the lack of diversity in the housing market presents a bleak picture for the changing demographic scene in the urban neighborhood environment. Family structures continue to transform in this neighborhood: single-parent households, couples, elderly, and the poor are faced with an urban housing stock that still caters to the modern nuclear-family scenario.

A Baptist church's parking lot is empty on most days of the week. On Sundays the congregation gathers and later departs. A fifteen-foot-wide easement along its eastern property line is dedicated to housing, offering a home for the local street prostitutes.

The southern rural housing typology, the shotgun house, is employed as the familiar beginning for the design of a seven-unit apartment building. The number seven is used for its sacred symbolism, to represent "the wholeness and completeness of all created things." [24] Stretching along the edge of the church lot, units are stacked three stories high in the fashion of one-over-one. At the rear of the property, a cloister is added to produce food and to provide a place of daily labor: tilling the soil to renew the spirit. The seven units share a common hall. Stairs are placed at the unit's corners, spiraling up to the top floor deck, a place to view the street and skyline. The western face of the housing is pierced with windows, constantly confronting the sacred, culminating at sunset, when the evening shadows move across the front of the building and set into the night.

Home for a Prostitute
Arriving home, she passes other studios
before arriving at her own. The sun is
bright as it sets over the bay. The church
seems larger in its silhouette. As she
undresses to shower, the shadow of the
steeple makes its way into her room.
For a brief moment she feels secure.

29th Street, Day Four: Home for a Prostitute

Removing my shirt and reaching into the shower, I remember how the marbled cocoa-butter soap bar disintegrated the day before. Turning the knob counter-clockwise, I return the gushing water to its drip and slip my shirt back on. Walking down to the corner store in the evening air renews my energy briefly. At the corner, a hand beckons for change, but my motion counters the exchange. Big Man is behind the counter. I circulate once and return to the counter. Big Man is busy with a customer. Old E, bologna, and three candy bars cross the counter between customer and owner. She is loud as she exclaims, "I'm short, you know I'm good." Big Man shrugs and bags the evening meal. With attentive eyes, he scans the store until I speak: "Do you have any soap?" "Over there," pointing to the far aisle. I browse somberly and only find two standard brands: Ivory and Dial. I ponder for an eternity and return with the carefully proportioned Ivory. My walk back to the counter involves passing a fully stocked cooler of malt liquor, two rows of standard canned and paper goods, and a barrage of candy and snack foods. Big Man rings up the Ivory, and I pay. As the bag crosses between us, Big Man shrugs. We go through it once again, as we do every time I find myself in this store. I ask him why he is killing my people with such a selection of goods in his "grocery store." He looks at me with a resigned eye. It is as if he knows my people are doomed. I step out into the dusk light.

Commerce

The neighborhood grocery store was a place where my mother would telephone biweekly orders and I would race the half mile to retrieve them. In those days, the trip to the store meant two-for-one cookies and the smell and sight of a man in a white apron behind the butcher counter. Today in West Oakland, the neighborhood store means malt liquor and cigarettes, beneficiaries of the corporate propaganda that fills the visual landscape of the inner city. When I smoked, people would ask why I smoked the brand Newport; my reply, "It was the only cigarette advertised in my neighborhood. The Marlboro man never visited."

The corner is a place to see and be seen. Next to the store, young and old stand around talking and watching the street. Every now and then someone will come along in a car and stop to talk. William Whyte describes the activities on the corner as "a great show and one of the best ways to make the most of it is, simply, not to wall it off." [25] This suggestion is typically ignored in inner-city communities where congregating on corners implies illicit activities and trouble. It's ironic that the same behavior in other areas of the city is encouraged and seen as a sign of vitality and community spirit.

The neighborhood store is a fixture that can spearhead change. The building is stripped bare and the transformation begins. The facade is broken open on the street side, bringing light into the small quarters. Liquor license reformation in neighborhoods will necessitate more creative marketing.

Neighborhood Store & Watchtower
Big Man awoke from his dream soaking wet. Visions of his regular customers walking towards him with small brown bags in their outstretched hands, bodies gaunt and malnourished. They were all over him, silhouettes screaming "killer," faceless shadows. He awakens to his responsibility to this community where he lives and works. The next day Big Man closed his store. Within a month he reopens with five types of soap, fresh produce, and a small deli. A black face can be seen through the once boarded-up window, standing behind the counter.

A deli counter is built along the rear wall, the aisle is widened, and the counter is positioned to view the entire store. Vegetable bins are movable indoors to outdoors. The corner receives an awning and chairs—a place to stop and chat and hang out. At night the steel doors roll down. Adjacent to the store, a market stall is set up with an overlook elevated high above the street, forming a new gateway. The overlook is an "imageable structure," [26] providing the street with an identity from within the community and to passersby. Here vegetables and other merchandise are sold by neighbors and merchants alike. The overlook is the nucleus for the street's neighborhood watch program, with neighbors taking their turns next to the neighborhood store.

It is Sarah's day to watch. She grabs her sketchbook and paints to pass the time; it is a great place to draw. She climbs the stair and relieves the morning shift. Miss Mabel tells her the day's events and a bit more before leaving. Sarah moves to her position in the neighborhood watchtower, sketchbook in hand. She nods to a merchant below, confirming that stall three is available. She looks down the street and smiles. Two kids look up and say hello as they race to the store.

29th Street, Day Five: Neighborhood Store and Watchtower

Martin Luther King Jr. Way

Starter Businesses

Programs for entrepreneurial aid in communities like West Oakland have spurred initiatives nationwide, including enterprise zones, small business minority loan programs, commercial incentive workshops and other revitalization measures. These economic assistance mechanisms are first-step attempts to encourage physical improvements and assist first-time and existing entrepreneurial venues. Many businesses are short-lived in West Oakland. In numerous cases, market studies, demographic profiles, and other necessary research are avoided, relying instead on popular fashion or marginal businesses which cater to the neighborhoods' economic and social ills. Physical streetscape improvements encourage new facade treatments and signage ordinances, nice paving, and adequate parking and site furnishings. They provide aesthetic relief.

These strategies all have merit, but they are only applicable to those who live within the community. The businesses that make it are quite idiosyncratic.

The Restaurant

This start-up business is inspired by the southern cooking tradition. The community currently hosts three, with a fourth added to Flints, Doug's, and Everett and Jones barbecue rib restaurants. To infuse novelty in the new business, a second feature is added: a detail shop (really a car wash). For those who have a penchant for southern cooking and a clean automobile, this proposal finds its niche.

The dual program starter business situates itself on a vacant corner lot along Martin Luther King Jr. Way. The building program is simple: two twenty-four foot by twenty-four foot buildings, wood frame construction and stucco, one red and the other yellow. The buildings are based on the "highway house" building typology. "Highway houses began with the shopkeeper-above-the-store mode as it was adapted to the selling of gasoline." [27] The rib crib and detail shop operates in this mixed-use mode, allowing the owners to live on the premises.

At the ground floor, the building's front twelve feet are driveway. The remaining twelve feet provide space for the office, the counter, the kitchen, and a waiting area. The second floor (twenty-four feet by twenty-four feet) overhangs the driveway, providing a full 864 square feet. The second-floor plan can accommodate two large living spaces or four small spaces. The rib crib needs no signage: its cooking hearth is a smoke shaft that rises up through the space. The landscape of the rib crib/detail shop consists of asphalt paving blocks and concrete. Sage borders the edges of the rib crib building, and lavender borders the detail shop. Each has a small rear yard with picnic tables for waiting customers.

Martin Luther King Jr. Way, Days One and Two: Rib Crib/Detail Shop

Day Three

Every time I go to Eli's, it always turns into an accountable experience. Kathi's and Chuck's arrival was just the reason to jam. Under the freeway seems a perfect place for a blues club—loud. I always feel nervous about leaving my car. One time I walked, but I can only do that with brothers and sisters. The place is filled as usual: always more whites than blacks. The dance floor is a cacophony of bouncy hippie-dancing and grooving. Troyce Keys just died—I guess his woman will keep the club going. He always played with everyone, just playing chord progressions. I wonder, will the tap dancing man be there? He is all over the place. He reminds me of Pop when he was a young man. That smile. Feeling good, feeling the blues.

Blues and Jazz

West Oakland was once the spot for music. "The commercial strip on West 7th Street, the 'main street' of West Oakland, flourished. Some of the biggest names in jazz and popular music, including Earl Fatha Hines, the Ink Spots, and Dinah Washington played in the jazz clubs there." [28] Historically, music has spilled out of the African American neighborhoods, providing a vibrant nightlife which reflects a cultural heritage and norm. But, as in many other cities, these institutions are now only part of the myths and histories that lie beneath the freeways and other infrastructure. In West Oakland today, the 7th Street corridor is musically silent; the only sounds are of trucks leaving the Bulk Mailing Facility and the rumble of the BART trains traversing the elevated track in the middle of 7th Street.

Blues Club

It seems appropriate for a culture's tradition and heritage to come to its aid in a time of crisis. It is also plausible for these products to come face-to-face with the instruments of their demise. The blues club is an advocate for this reconciliation. Physically, the blues club is a new machine in the West Oakland landscape. It is sited a half block away from the successful blues venue, Eli's Mile High Club, which sits in the shadow of the MacArthur Freeway and I-980 interchange. The new club is placed underneath the ramps.

Constructed of concrete and steel, the club is a large acoustic box. The main entry, located on Martin Luther King Jr. Way, features a blue concrete wall. A gridded mosaic of blue hues creates a visual display. At different positions and levels, various grids can be pulled down to provide seats and musical stages. Like lines on a music score, the occupation of the wall is improvisational. The overhead freeway ramps provide an acoustical roof for the wailing sounds to reverberate.

The club's roof is a major signature. A steel portico rises up to the freeway ramp, cloaking its presence along the axis of Martin Luther King Jr. Way. The steel reflects light and sky, and it signals the gateway to the new music district. Its concrete pilotis (as in the Johnson Wax Building) dance in space as they support the gigantic ceiling overhead.

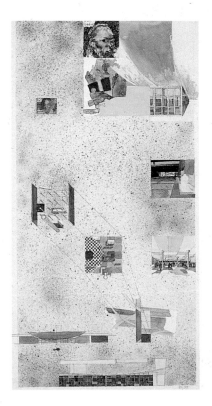

Blues Club

By day the sound of a sax can be heard, emanating from beneath the overpass. Musicians practice along the blue hinged wall. Their sound is all sweet—quieting and containing the roar from above. Young and old dance or sway to their riffs. When night falls over the city, the underpass is lit. A magical blue shadow invites people in to dance and hear the new Oakland sound. The columns join them. Barrettes, hats, and dreadlocks glow from the checkered dance floor. Dance man, how sweet.

Martin Luther King Jr. Way, Day Three: Blues Club

Day Four

*His truck is parked at the same corner
on most afternoons in the summer. He is
leaning against the truck speaking to the
woman who lives on the corner. The
fruits and vegetables are in full view to
cars and passersby. There never is a real
gathering of customers to buy his goods.
Just a few older residents who seem to be
longtime acquaintances. Still, day in and
day out, he comes. Maybe one day they
will see him.*

Vendors

Street vendors provide commerce and
entertainment on city streets in Berkeley,
California, Santa Fe, New Mexico, and
Greenwich Village in New York. Street
life in those places revolves around
buyers and sellers. Many places require
a license. In return, the city does little to
assist this hybrid activity. Sidewalks and
streets cater primarily to auto use. Site
infrastructure that supports economic
activity is usually temporary. Carts, boards,
and tables disappear with the street
merchants, returning the streets to their
primary purpose.

What would happen if the streets were
given over to citizens for daily marketing
and selling? Would the "Ramblas" or
"bizarre" unfold?

Selling Boxes

Stationed at curbside along the street,
vendor boxes are installed by the city
for public entrepreneurial opportunities.
You can lease the boxes for a small daily
fee. Once you make a deposit at City
Hall, you are given a key to the box of
your choice and location. The hours
of operation are 7:00 A.M. to 7:00 P.M.

The boxes are fabricated out of steel and
bronze. By night, they are autonomous
fixtures along the street. By day, steel arms
are raised up for business. The outer
walls operate on hinges. Once unlocked,
they tilt towards the sky, revealing
display space, electrical hookups, and
a hose bib.

Selling Boxes

*He pulls up at curbside in his Ford truck.
The largest sign on his camper shell reads
"Do You Love Jesus?" Once outside,
he inspects the selling boxes' sizes and
capacities. After a few moments, he returns
to the truck and removes a medium-sized
box filled with religious pamphlets and
books. He arranges them neatly on the
shelves, stepping back on occasion to make
sure each is visible. After meticulously
arranging the literature, he returns to
the truck and pulls away from the curb.
Looking back through the rear view
mirror he sees a young man approach
the selling booth.*

Martin Luther King Jr. Way, Day Four: Selling Boxes

Epilogue

Many of these proposals transgress the boundaries of normative societal attitudes toward neighborhoods and open spaces. They validate "familiar" activities, events, and patterns of life without applying moral judgments. Kevin Lynch in 1965 wrote: "We should design for diversity, experiment with new types, open recreational choices, fit opportunities to the real diversity." [29] The miniparks of West Oakland await the opportunity to express real diversity.

As research, these urban diaries have raised hard questions. These questions need to be asked if open spaces are to accommodate diversity and play a significant role in the lives of the people who reside here in West Oakland. The same is true in any other urban landscape. This research does not attempt to solve problems but to make them visible.

The questions that arise from this research are essential concerns and must be addressed by any designer who approaches open spaces/public spaces in urban areas. These questions include:

In this era of standardization, how do we expect to reflect and serve diversity in the landscape?

Can open spaces be the sole savior of neighborhoods facing economic, social, and physical decline?

Is it possible for there to be a nonjudgmental design?

By understanding different cultural patterns and practices, how can new meanings be generated so that they are reflected in the landscape?

Can physical design solutions continue to transform and reshape themselves as their surroundings are transformed?

End of the diaries.

Album

Photography by Walter Hood

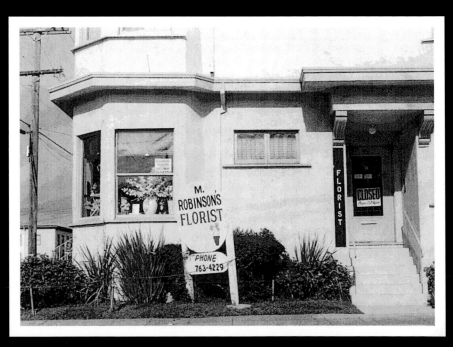

Old E, bologna, and three candy bars cross the counter between customer and owner.

The dance floor is a cacophony of bouncing, hippie-dancing, and grooving. Troyce Keys just died.

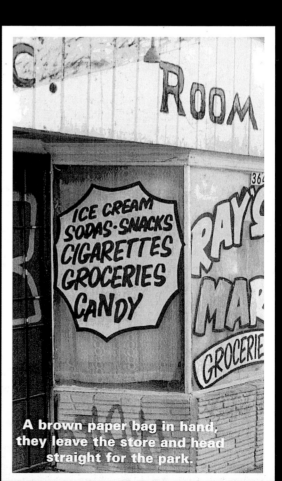

A brown paper bag in hand, they leave the store and head straight for the park.

No matter how dark it gets, there are always small glimmers of life that feed hope, that show endurance.

BUSINESS HOURS

MON. CLOSED
TUE. CLOSED
WED. CLOSED
THU. 7pm TO 2am
FRI. 7pm TO 2am
SAT. 7pm TO 2am
SUN. 7pm TO 2am

655-6661

NO
LOITERING

C.P.C. 647-E

GROVE STREET
BIBLE WAY CHURCH

Sundays always feel like Sundays.

Leah Levy

Leah Levy is an independent art curator and writer living in Berkeley, California. She studied the history of art at Simmons College and Tufts University in Massachusetts, and was the Director of the Parker Street 470 Gallery, the seminal Boston gallery of large-scale painting and sculpture, in the early 1970s. From 1974-1983, she owned and directed the Leah Levy Gallery in San Francisco. As founding curator of Capp Street Project, the internationally recognized artist-in-residency program in San Francisco, she worked with artists including James Turrell, David Ireland and Mary Lucier. In 1989, she was appointed Trustee of the Estate of the artist Jay DeFeo.

Ms. Levy wrote the essay and text for *Peter Walker: Minimalist Gardens*, published by Spacemaker Press in 1997.

Lewis Watts

Lewis Watts is a photographer based in the San Francisco Bay Area. He teaches Photography and Visual Studies in the College of Environmental Design at the University of California, Berkeley. The images in *Urban Diaries* are part of a larger "cultural landscape" series that explores evidence of life experience in rural and urban African American Environments. Work by Lewis Watts has been published widely and exhibited internationally.

Notes

1. Herbert Blumer, *Symbolic Interactionism: Perspective and Method* (Englewood Cliffs, New Jersey: Prentice Hall, 1969).

2. Christian Norberg-Schultz, *Architecture, Meaning and Place* (New York: Rizzoli International Publications, 1988).

3. Lars Lerup, *Building the Unfinished: Architecture and Human Action* (Beverly Hills and London: Sage Library of Social Research, 1977).

4. Galen Cranz, *The Politics of Open Space Design* (Cambridge: Massachusetts Institute of Technology Press, 1982).

5. Randolph Hester, *Planning Neighborhood Space* (New York: Van Nostrand Reinhold, 1984).

6. Thomas Angotti, *Metropolis 2000, Planning, Poverty and Politics* (New York: Routledge Press, 1993).

7. Lawrence Crouchett, Lonnie G. Bunch III, and Martha Kendall Winnacker, *Visions Towards Tomorrow: The History of the East Bay Afro-American Community, 1852-1977* (Oakland: Northern California Center for African American History and Life, 1989).

8. Douglas Henry Daniels, *Pioneer Urbanites: A Social and Cultural History of Black San Francisco* (Philadelphia: Temple University Press, 1980).

9. See note 8 above.

10. See note 7 above.

11. Melvin Mogulof, "Black Community Development in Five Western Model Cities," *Social Work* 15 (1970).

12. See note 6 above.

13. Jane Jacobs, *The Death and Life of Great American Cities* (New York: Random House, 1961).

14. Bruce Stokes, *Helping Ourselves: Local Solutions to Global Problems* (New York: W.W. Norton and Co., 1981).

15. Lerup uses the term "lump" to refer to the way a culture reduces an object to a one-dimensional concept. In fact, the object often is a single lump of material. See note 3 above, p. 128.

16. Mark Rios, "Redefining the Idea of Play," *Landscape Architecture Magazine* (Washington, D.C.: American Society of Landscape Architecture, 1994).

17. Steven Holl, *Rural and Urban House Types in North America* (New York: Pamphlet Architecture, 1982).

18. See note 7 above.

19. See note 5 above.

20. See note 13 above.

21. Speaking of "environmental fortuna," Lerup quotes Heidegger, who says that : "in order to know an object we must embrace, study, all its sides." Lerup explains that, "Once some or all of its sides are revealed, prompted, or discovered, the object is potentially more useful to us in our every day lives. For to discover the possible many-sidedness of an object is to reveal its opportunity— what I call environmental fortuna." (*Building the Unfinished*: 129).

22. Donald Appleyard, *Livable Streets* (Berkeley: University of California Press, 1981). Appleyard's seven points include the street as: 1. safe sanctuary, 2. livable, healthy environment, 3. community, 4. neighborhood territory, 5. place to play and learn, 6. green and pleasant land, 7. unique historic place.

23. Paul Groth, "Vernacular Parks," in *Denatured Visions: Landscape and Culture in the Twentieth Century* (New York: Museum of Modern Art, 1991).

24. Lorna Price, *The Plan of St. Gall in Brief* (Berkeley: University of California Press, 1982).

25. William Whyte, The *Social Life of Small Urban Spaces* (New York: William Whyte, 1980).

26. Kevin Lynch, *Image of the City* (Cambridge: Massachusetts Institute of Technology Press, 1960). Lynch defines imageability as the "quality in a physical object which gives it a high probability of evoking a strong image in any given observer. It is that shape, color or arrangement which facilitates the making of vividly identified, powerfully structured, highly useful mental images of the environment."

27. See note 17 above.

28. Elizabeth Bagwell, *Oakland: The Story of a City* (Novato, California: Presidio Press, 1982).

29. Kevin Lynch, "City as Environment," in *Cities* (New York: Scientific American, 1965).